THE Easter Story

First published in 2003 by Evans Brothers Ltd.
2A Portman Mansions, Chiltern Street, London W1U 6NR

Text copyright © 2001 Anita Ganeri
Illustrations copyright © 2003 Evans Brothers Ltd.

The text of *The Easter Story* is based on *The Story of Easter*, one of nine stories first published in *Christian Stories*, a title in the *Storyteller* series published by Evans Brothers Ltd.

Editor: Louise John
Designer: Simon Borrough
Illustrations: Rachael Phillips, Allied Artists
Production: Jenny Mulvanny
Consultants: Alan Brown

Published in the United States by Smart Apple Media
1980 Lookout Drive, North Mankato, Minnesota 56003

Library of Congress Cataloging-in-Publication Data

Ganeri, Anita, 1961–
The Easter story / Anita Ganeri ; illustrated by Rachael Phillips. p. cm.
Summary: Introduces the events leading up to the death of Jesus and his resurrection, describing how these events are celebrated by Christians. Includes the Lord's Prayer and instructions for decorating Easter eggs.
ISBN 1-58340-488-0
1. Jesus Christ—Resurrection—Juvenile literature. 2. Jesus Christ—Passion—
Juvenile literature. [1. Jesus Christ—Passion. 2. Jesus Christ—Resurrection. 3. Easter.] I. Phillips, Rachael, ill. II. Title.

BT482.G36 2004
232.9'7—dc22 2003058991

9 8 7 6 5 4 3 2 1

Acknowledgments:
For permission to reproduce copyright material,
the author and publishers gratefully acknowledge the following:
page 20 Trip/M. Fairman
page 21 Trip/M. Jelliffe

THE Easter Story

Anita Ganeri

Illustrated by
Rachael Phillips

A⁺

Contents

At the time of the festival of Passover, Jesus traveled to Jerusalem with his disciples. He knew that his life was in danger, for there were many priests and leaders in Jerusalem who did not like what he taught. They saw him as a threat to their power and authority. But the ordinary people of the city flocked to see him.

As Jesus rode into the city on the back of a donkey, crowds of people lined the street to greet him. Some spread their cloaks on the ground in front of him. Others waved long branches of palm leaves.

"Hosanna in the highest!" they shouted.

"Blessed is he that comes in the name of the Lord."

It was a welcome fit for any king.

A few days later, Jesus sat down with his disciples to share a Passover feast. It should have been a happy occasion, but Jesus had important things to say.

"This is the last meal we will share together," he told the astonished disciples.

Then he picked up some bread, blessed it, and broke it into pieces.

"Eat this bread," he said. "This is to remind you of me."

Then he poured a cup of wine and passed it around for all of them to share.

"Drink this wine," he said. "This is to remind you that my blood will be shed for you."

The disciples did what Jesus asked. But they did not understand why Jesus had said that this would be their last meal together. Then Jesus said, "One of you sitting here will betray me."

The disciples were stunned. They could not believe their ears. They loved Jesus very much. Why would any of them want to betray him?

Quietly, Simon Peter asked, "Lord, who will it be?"

Jesus did not reply, but he took a piece of bread and dipped it in some wine. Then he handed it to Judas and said, "Go and do what you have to do."

Jesus knew that his enemies had offered Judas 30 pieces of silver to betray his master.

Judas rushed out of the room.

Later that night, Jesus went with the disciples to the Garden of Gethsemane on the Mount of Olives. He asked the disciples to stay awake with him while he prayed. While they were there, Judas led the soldiers to him.

"The man I kiss is the one you want," Judas whispered to the soldiers. Then he went up to Jesus and kissed him.

At once, the soldiers grabbed Jesus and arrested him. They led him first to the priests, who accused him of telling lies about being the Son of God, and then they spat on him and threw him into prison.

The next day, the soldiers took Jesus to the Roman governor, Pontius Pilate, who sentenced him to death. Jesus was taken to a place called Golgotha—the Place of the Skull—where he was nailed to a cross and left to die.

"Forgive them, Father," Jesus prayed through his pain. "For they do not understand what they are doing."

Later that day, Jesus died.

Some of Jesus's close friends lifted his body
gently down from the cross and wrapped it in a
white robe. Then they placed it in a tomb cut
out of rock. With heavy hearts, they rolled a
stone across the entrance and wept. They
thought that they would never see Jesus again.

Three days later, Jesus's friends returned to the tomb. An amazing sight met their eyes. The stone had been rolled away, and Jesus's body was gone! An angel, shining with light, stood beside the empty tomb. Before they could find their voices, the angel spoke:

"Don't be afraid," the angel said. "I know that you are looking for Jesus. But he is not here. He has risen from the dead and come back to life."

Jesus's friends were filled with hope and joy. But they were also worried. The news seemed too good to be true. How could Jesus have come back to life after they had seen him die?

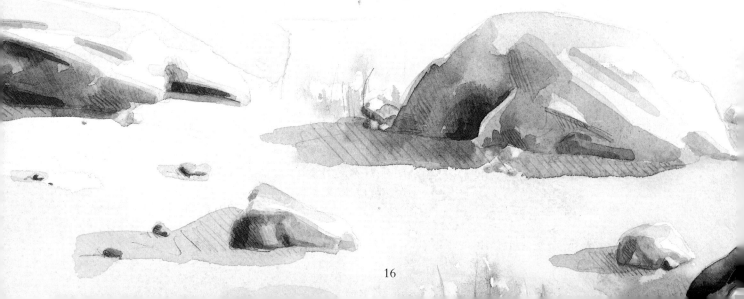

But as they ran to tell the others what they had seen and heard, a man stood in their path. The man was Jesus!

Jesus told them not to be afraid and to tell his friends to go to Galilee, where they would see him.

Every year at Easter, Christians remember Jesus's death. Because Jesus died on a Friday, the day is called Good Friday and is a sad time. Jesus rose from the dead on the following Sunday, Easter Day. This is a happy time for Christians, when they give thanks to God for Jesus's life. Christians believe that Jesus died to save people from their sins. They believe that Jesus rose from the dead and is with God forever. This is called the Resurrection.

Holy Communion

Today, nearly all Christians still share bread and wine together as part of their worship, just as the disciples did at the Last Supper. In this way, they remember the last meal that Jesus ate with his disciples. This service is often called Holy Communion or Mass. The bread and wine are blessed by the priest or minister. Sharing the bread and wine helps Christians to feel closer to God.

The Christian Cross

The cross is a very important symbol for Christians. It reminds them of Jesus's death and the Resurrection.

A crucifix is a cross with the figure of Jesus on it, to show how he died. A plain cross does not have a figure

on it. This shows that Jesus has risen from the dead. Jesus suffered five wounds when he was nailed to the cross. A plain cross sometimes has five jewels on it to represent these wounds.

The Lord's Prayer

This is the most important Christian prayer. Jesus taught it to his disciples when they asked him how they should pray.

Our Father, who art in Heaven,
Hallowed be thy name.
Thy kingdom come,
Thy will be done,
On Earth as it is in Heaven.
Give us this day our daily bread,
And forgive us our trespasses
As we forgive those that trespass against us.
And lead us not into temptation
But deliver us from evil.
For thine is the kingdom,
The power, and the glory,
For ever and ever.
Amen

Making Painted Easter Eggs

Join in the fun of Easter and try making these painted eggs.

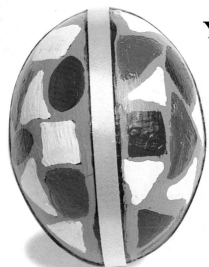

You will need:
- some fresh eggs
- bright, thick paints and a
- paintbrush
- decorations (such as sequins)
- craft glue

What to do:

1. Ask an adult to cook an egg until it is hard–boiled and then let it cool. Or, ask an adult to make a small hole at each end of an egg for you. Blow the inside of the egg out through one of the holes, then let the shell dry.

2. Paint the egg with bright colors and patterns. You will need to put on more than one coat of paint to make the colors really bright.

3. Decorate the egg. Use the glue to attach sequins and other decorations.

**If you enjoyed this book,
why not read *The Christmas Story*?**

The story of the birth of Jesus is beautifully told and richly
illustrated in *The Christmas Story*. The book also includes additional
information about Christmas, the words and music to a favorite
carol, "Away in a Manger," and a delicious Christmas recipe.